PAIN SO UTTER

A DICKINSON INSPIRED
COLLECTION OF POEMS

NILANJANA DAS BARMAN

Copyright © Nilanjana Das Barman
All Rights Reserved.

This book has been published with all efforts taken to make the material error-free after the consent of the author. However, the author and the publisher do not assume and hereby disclaim any liability to any party for any loss, damage, or disruption caused by errors or omissions, whether such errors or omissions result from negligence, accident, or any other cause.

While every effort has been made to avoid any mistake or omission, this publication is being sold on the condition and understanding that neither the author nor the publishers or printers would be liable in any manner to any person by reason of any mistake or omission in this publication or for any action taken or omitted to be taken or advice rendered or accepted on the basis of this work. For any defect in printing or binding the publishers will be liable only to replace the defective copy by another copy of this work then available.

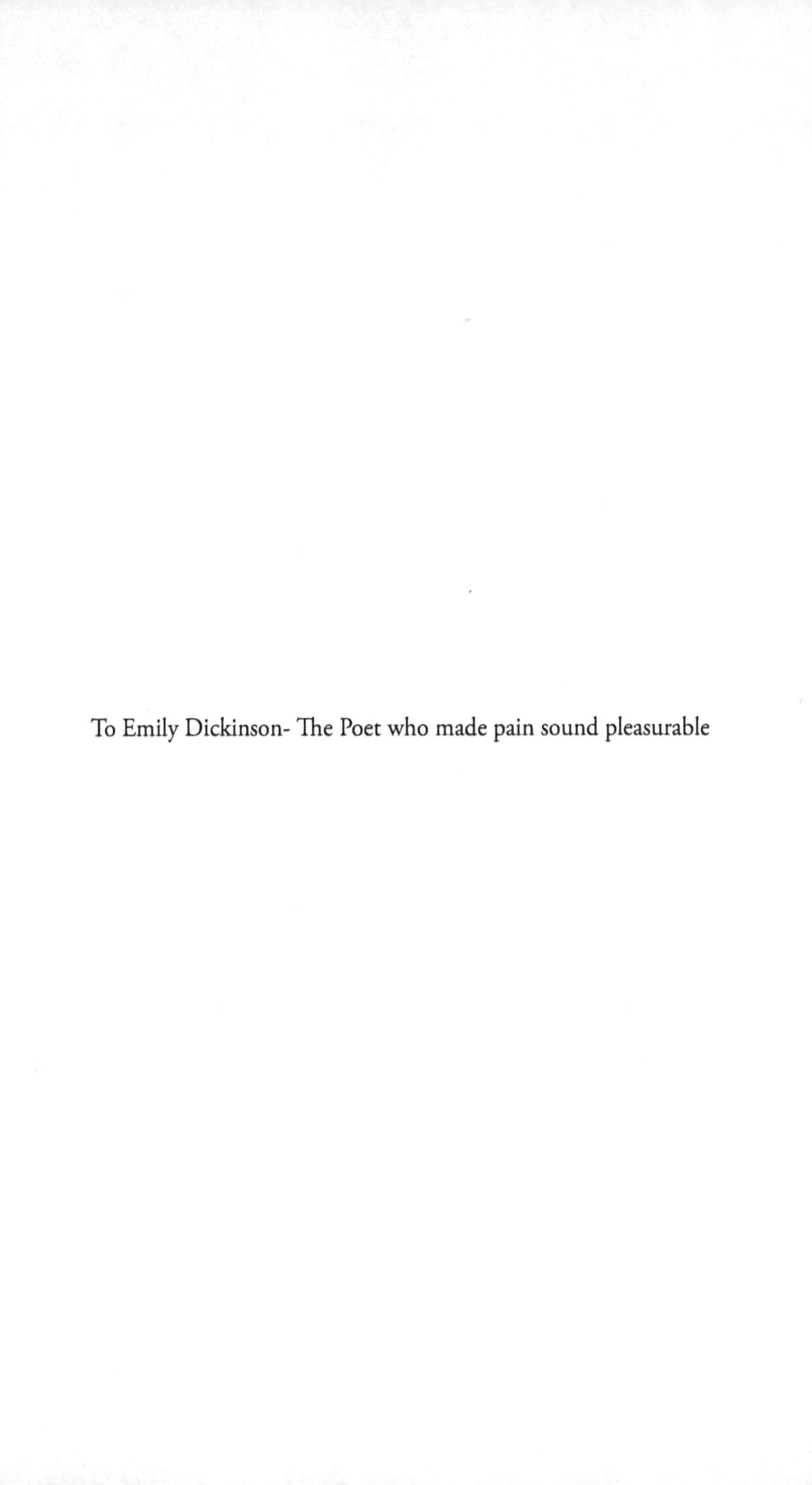

To Emily Dickinson- The Poet who made pain sound pleasurable

Contents

Preface

There is a pain — so utter —

It swallows substance up —

Then covers the Abyss with Trance —

So Memory can step

Around — across — opon it —

As One within a Swoon —

Goes safely — where an open eye —

Would drop Him — Bone by Bone —

-Emily Dickinson

Emily Dickinson is often considered one of the pioneers of modern poetry along with Walt Whitman. Pain so utter is a tribute to her contribution to the world of poetry. Several of her poems revolved around the themes of pain and death. However none of her poems were gloomy in any way. During her lifetime she published only ten poems and a letter. Most of her writings were unveiled after her death which created a ripple in the world of poetry that contintues till this day.

Pain So Utter is a tribute to her writing and includes a collection of twenty one poems inspired by her.

Acknowledgements

I must thank those who are on the journey with me right now. I thank my better half who is a constant encouragement in my walk of faith and with whom I hope to share eternity in heaven. I thank my friends and colleagues who have encouraged me in ways they do not even realize. And I thank my family for accepting me as I am. Many teachers came in my journey in faith, and I must acknowledge the contribution of each and everyone. But as I do it all I must thank Jesus for this life, this purpose, and His love.

Lastly, I would also like to thank you, the reader who picked up this book and believed in me!

1. Who are you?

I fail to recognize-
Who are you?
A spectre,
Resurrected,
From a grave of
Expectations,
Broken,
Forgotten,
Unbidden,
Zombies of
Autocracy-
A remnant,
Lingering past
The hour of
Forgetfulness.

2. Boxes of Concrete

The boxes reinforced
With grey concrete,
Frozen and fluid,
Confine wings of
Despondency.

Angels engraved in stone,
Are still stone,
Perched on a tombstone,
That witness a life
In death.

Spears pointing
Accusations
Amplify desperation,
Vanity suffocating,
Within mortar and bricks.

You fit me
Where I do not fit,
As you limit,
My bones twisted
To fit your skeleton.

Yet my rubber appendages,
Bounce to the whim
Of your eccentricities,
A mannequin I will be,
Of propriety.

Microfractures in concrete,
Reveal fissures,
Ideologies rupture.
I am no more me
No more a thing of beauty.

Rivulets oozing
Of essence,
Fragrant and acrid.
Retched from the corpse
Embalmed but sentient.

3. Stain on Silk

Torn pages stained with ink
Illegible and unintelligible.
Secrets crackling in a fire,
Soot and flames burn,
Amidst smoke and tears.
Histories repeat,
On silken beds,
And in dingy motels.
Fairies do not tell tales,
Of broken promises.
Secrets run up the stream,
Afraid of drowning
In a sea of lies.
Every shore
Scribbles loud goodbyes.
Sore lips often taste
A bit like toffee,
Chewy till the liquid
Oozes out-
Salty drops-
Regret clothed in a hurry,
Mistakes guise as redress,
Peeking under skirts,

Too short, too flailed.

4. Pillows

Amidst the grime of nights-
Unkempt-
Tears gather,
A glacier inside a frozen heart,
Waiting for a summer
That is yet to come.

There are currents
Flowing under-
Some strong,
Sweeping the Westerlies,
Off track
Just by the faintest touch.

Some rivulets imprint lines,
Washed eyeliners
Come dime a dozen.
There are grassland
Amidst briny desert winds,
Fed by soaked pillows
Watered in lonely nights.

5. Today

Seconds melt into hours,
Days find a rhythm
To transpose and fuse
With the Universe that moves-

Expanding bit by bit
The planets revolve and sway,
Tomorrow is a myth
For those standing at the precipice.

Home is a moment-
Suspended and stoic,
Held in a vacant gaze
That justifies an existence.

Time often stands still,
Though clocks chime and tick-
Tomorrow is a myth
To the believers of today.

6. The Shadow

It fell under the Juniper
Like Medusa's flowing hair
Reaching into the hearts
Of the brave that would dare.
Writhing past ragged rocks,
It climbed with thirsting hours,
Blooming in the darkness,
That spoke of putrid flowers.
The rafflesia bled in purple
As flies hovered in a swarm,
The mountains beyond are stoic,
Though the stream beneath is warm.
And life creeps on slowly,
Haustoria thrust in deep,
Drinking from fissures
Feeding on heart that weep.
The oceans taste of iron,
Wreckage lost in time.
Lost city of Atlantis
Amidst corals sublime.
And yet stretch the shadow,
Of desolation and despair.
Death! O so faithful,

Eternity beyond so fair.

7. My cage

I build my cage
With an iron frame
Cast in my cold
Indifference.

They were shaped
By and by.
You saw it not,
As they welded.

Perhaps it traps
My whims and wills
But I am safe
From predators large.

My cage I build
And find wings clipped.
Do you have feathers,
I can glue to me?

My cage still stands,
And I peer out.
The blue skies

Are no different now.

The eagle soars
Just as high.
There are the clouds
And here am I.

8. Refrain

I stop myself
In the nick of time,
Before I said another sorry.
Apologies
Are part of life
But often they make me wary.

Oftentimes-
I apologize
For my very being.
And then I find
A silent room,
Confining but freeing.

I am sorry for
The countless hours,
I spend in self control.
I am sorry for
The days spent
Rising from my fall.

With wings meant to
Soar high

I take a plunge so deep.
I have a cipher-
Within my bosom,
My and my to keep.

I am sorry for
The locked door-
The sealed window shut.
I want to show
The world my home
But I stumble at the but-

I am sorry for
The apology
It may not be enough.
But my selfish truant ego
Is made of
Stronger stuff.

You never guess
But my list of worries
Don't always mean regret.
Perhaps to you,
My absent remorse,
Is a cause to be upset.

I am sorry that

Your keen eyes
Often miss my tears.
I am sorry that
Your frowning brows,
Oft be the cause of my fears.

I am sorry that
I cannot tell you,
Exactly when I'm sorry.
I am sorry that
I can't help but make
You a point of worry.

But then again
One fine day
I will come and apologize.
My words won't be
A controlled refrain,
Your eyes wills show surprise.

I am sorry that
It's not today,
And you see a different me.
I am sorry that
Even though uncaged,
I long to be free.

9. The Grave

It's empty now,
But not forever,
To be emptied
Forevermore.
Bones to fossils,
Flesh to dust,
Soul to Supersoul.
Resurrected and
Transfigured,
Defying gravity.
The Grave will open
Once forever
And heavens will
Bow and sing-

It's not empty now
But soon will be
As flesh cover
Dry bones.
Red to pink,
Then turning paler,
Pall to skin it goes.
Breath is breathed

The molecule at a time,
As deflated lungs
Restore.
Though occupied,
But with hope,
The fish lands ashore.

10. My Garden

Lilies encircled
By morose moths,
Sunflowers sunbathing.
Bougianvillas surrounded by
Butterflies ever fading-
Welcome to my garden
With petunias to please.
Roses scheming in broad daylight,
Hibiscus singing to bees.
And amidst it all, I sit,
The scarecrow that fails to scare.
With my scissors, I prune and snip,
Without emotion or care.
The show I put is a good one,
Because inside I bleed,
At every prick and every cut,
At every wilted seed.
Welcome to my garden
Amidst the smell of manure,
The money plant twisting haustoria
The sage speaking of a cure.
And amidst it, all the skies turn blue,
And sometimes green and red.

And amidst my garden
Remains a patch,
That one day maybe my bed.
With roots this deep I will spread,
My haustoria and my leaves.
Welcome to my garden,
Infested with moths and bees.

11. Home

Tied in a ribbon-
Wrapped in satin-
Red and white,
White and red-

The keys jingle in the wind-
A storm approaching-
Windows straining to keep-
Adversity at bay-

My home is a refuge-
Made of ancient wood-
Stained with blood-
Pierced with nails-

A tower I build-
With broken tiles-
With transparent windows-
And a naked brick wall-

My home stands,
Against the hail-
The sunbeam attacks,

Fierce but slant-

I make a home-
Amidst dry bones-
I dig a grave-
I water my plants.

12. Pencil

Sharp like a blade-
Blade against wood-
Pointed and black-
Charcoal and clay-

Sharp like a needle-
Drawing red blood-
Bent with use-
Metal and bone-

Shaped like an art-
A crafted fine tip-
Made to glide-
Over a bleached white page-

Everything comes down-
To the stroke of a line-
A pencil it remains-
Even when it glides-
On a naked pall-

13. Whispers

Whispers of the night bid goodbye-
The morning sun does not greet.
I feel like a pariah
In the embrace of a breeze,
That sees not-
The darkness or the light.

Howlings of a wild wind-
Comes floating on wispy clouds-
The breeze murmurs a lullaby-
Its voice is too harsh-
To sing me to sleep.

The willows mumble
Of a night that was-
The old oak grumbles a
About the had been-
I looked expectantly
To a darkened horizon-
All I receive
Are ominous visions-

14. The Prophet

The old frail prophet
Hunched under a tree-
Whispers to himself-
Like any other lunatic-

He tells of destruction-
And the world falling down-
We wait and wait-
Till in relief, we breathe-

The old frail prophet
Still whispers curses-
Hoping of death-
Smelling of defeat-

We drink and are merry-
We sing for joy-
The old frail prophet-
Grumbles inside me-

15. Surrender

There is something about surrender
That makes it absolute.

Giving reign over your soul,
Branding it, to be used.

You take it as my weakness,
But it gives me a sense of power.

As I can let go of control,
For hour after hour,

A power that brands,
Like tongues of raining fire,

Falling down from heaven
To grace the praying tower.

And kneeling I pray,
Standing I surmise,

On every moment spent
As your victorious prize.

Like a coal-burning,
Dimly desire burns,

Heaping grace upon grace,
Till the heart is won.

It is never about the flesh,
The senses skin to skin,

It's never about the skin,
Neither righteousness nor sin.

Control holds its breath
Through sparks, eyes can't see

Surrender is a treasure-
With a map buried under the sea-

16. Detachment

I hate you in my detachment
Because you deserve not my hate.
There are chasms drawn out,
Amidst shattered monuments
Destined to symbolize
Immortality and our joined fates.

I choose to unshackle the horses,
Send to rot in your dungeon fair,
And ride them to the far end,
Away from lies and despair.

I hate you in my absence,
One that you're bound to feel.
An absence that I sorely need
To recuperate and heal.

17. The Bouquet

Dead people receive more flowers than living ones
Ans the living ones are not there to water the dead flowers
Wilting on graves unattended
After the funeral service is over.
It takes a while for it to be cleaned,
And till then death rots,
Like a shallow grave dug out in haste,
A body put in a coffin to forget,
Time is not partial to the living.

Dead people receive more respect than the living,
Especially dried bones, shrivelled with age,
Left alone to years of neglect,
A Christmas postcard that never reaches.
The Grim Reaper brings many friends,
People to shed tears over a broken shell,
Eulogies talk about legends and myths,
The soul suffocates amidst empty walls.

Dead people have more to give than the living
And it is not just the will bequeathed to he lost.
Lessons learnt are recounted in memories.
Many lessons are whispered as myths.

Stories are made up of headstones,
In abandoned graveyards that no one visits,
And yet that odd passerby comes,
Holding a bouquet that the living does not get.
Death is the start of every religion.
How many prayed before the first death?
Before the first loss did how many care?
And yet death is the end of it all.

Dead people lead the living to live,
Through whispered prayers and faith unseen,
Dead people receive more flowers,
Because flowers bloom from emptied dreams.

18. Time

What is time if not life-
An expansion: slow.
The opening of a bud,
In the early morning dew-
Gradual, but sure;
Till all is lost
In the coming snow.
Dust meets dust,
And the sands of time-
Flows.

From one end to the other,
Running between galaxies,
Universe collides into
Inevitability.

19. Remembered

Etched by acid
On a copper plate
Buried deep inside-
Excavated
At the edge of time
To reveal secrets-

What secrets are kept
In moments sealed
In the amber of yesterday?
Frozen air bubbles encapsulated
In immortalized dreams!

Days turn to memory-
Remembered
Now and then.

20. Backspace Wins

I have lost touch with reality often,
Before hitting that button,
Which erases all eccentricities,
Allowing you to fit in.

Normal isn't overrated,
Not yet,
Though I wish hard that it was.
The spacing in my letter,

Or the level of propriety,
It is hard to be adequate,
When you aim to be outstanding.

The word outstanding
Start with an 'O'
Which isn't much orgasmic,
Not like that bite
Into a bar of dark chocolate.

TMI: Too much information.
That is what it's for,
The backspace button.

I like venting into my journal,
Not that paper one.
There it's etched in stone,
Or rather paper.
150 GSM of inappropriate,
But hard-hitting facts.

I prefer my hits small,
If only I had a choice.
The backspace is the only button,
I hit harder than I should,

Harder and faster my fingers go.
So much friction-
The paper would catch fire.

You look at me and rarely know,
What I have erased when sober.
Because the censure is rational,
Not me, not often.

The secrets are scandalous,
Sometimes,
When no one looks.
Whenever needed
I hit that one long button.

Harder and faster,
Backspace wins.

21. Shall We Talk?

Let us sit now in the shade of the poplar,
In the summer evening breeze.
Let us descend into a camaraderie
With familiarity and ease.

Let's talk about the fall of Athens,
And the rise of yonder sun.
Let's surmise on Armaggeddon,
Or where life first began.

Let us sit down for an aeon,
Or a fraction of an hour.
Let's talk about oblivion
Or just tell me your favourite flower.

Let us sit and then dance,
Around the issue at hand,
The elephant in the room,
The monster in the sand.